THE TRAVELER'S SIMPLE PATTERN COLORING BOOK

BY

ALISON COOKSEY

ISBN-13:
978-1532821646
ISBN-10:
1532821646

COLOR TEST PAGE

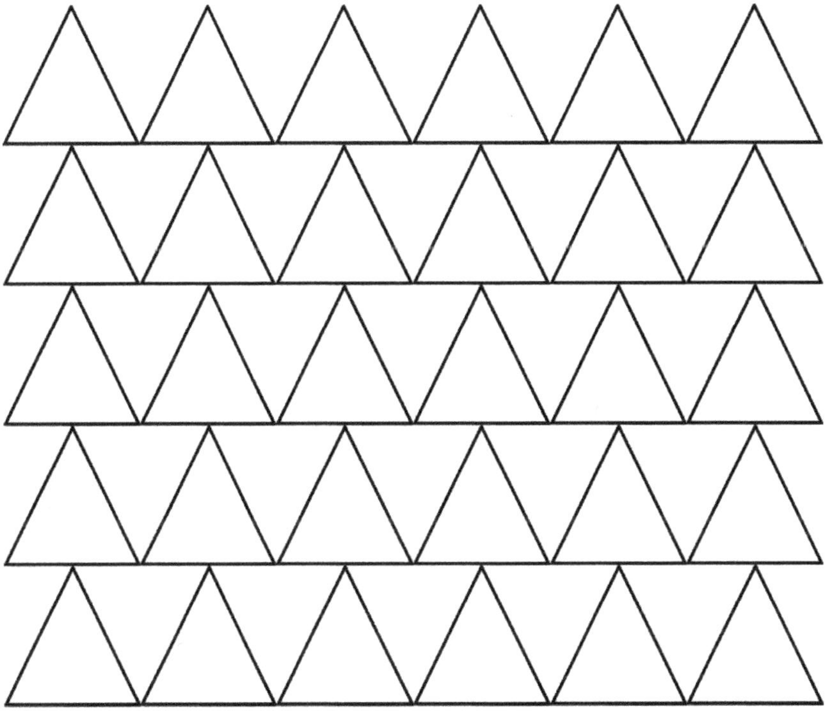

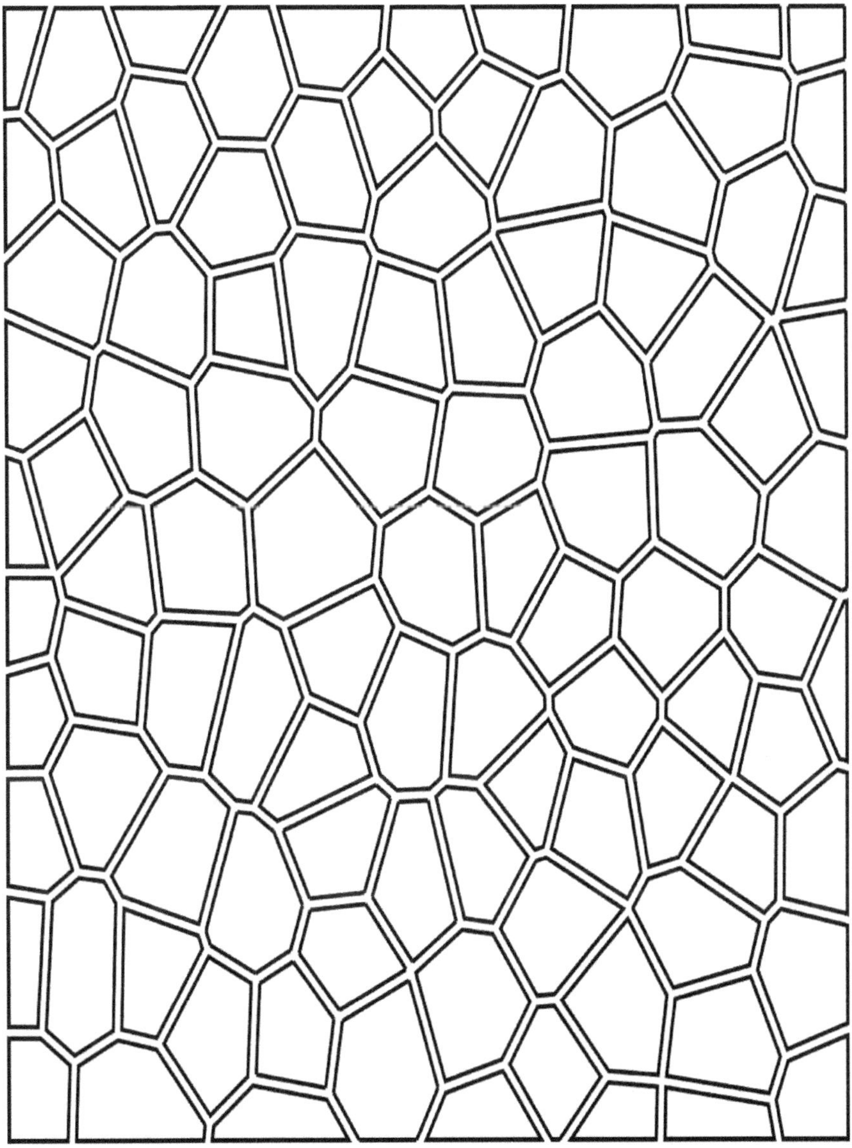

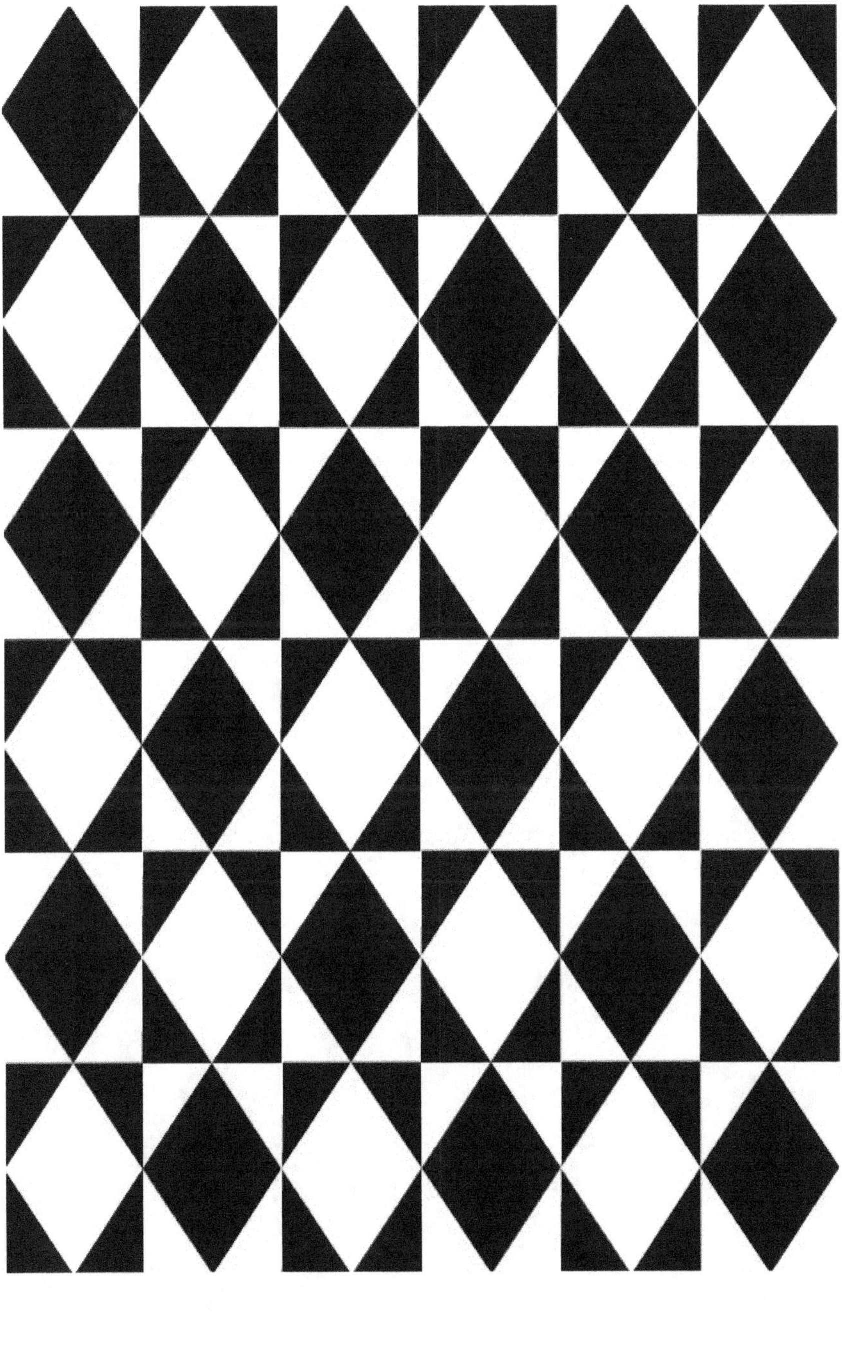

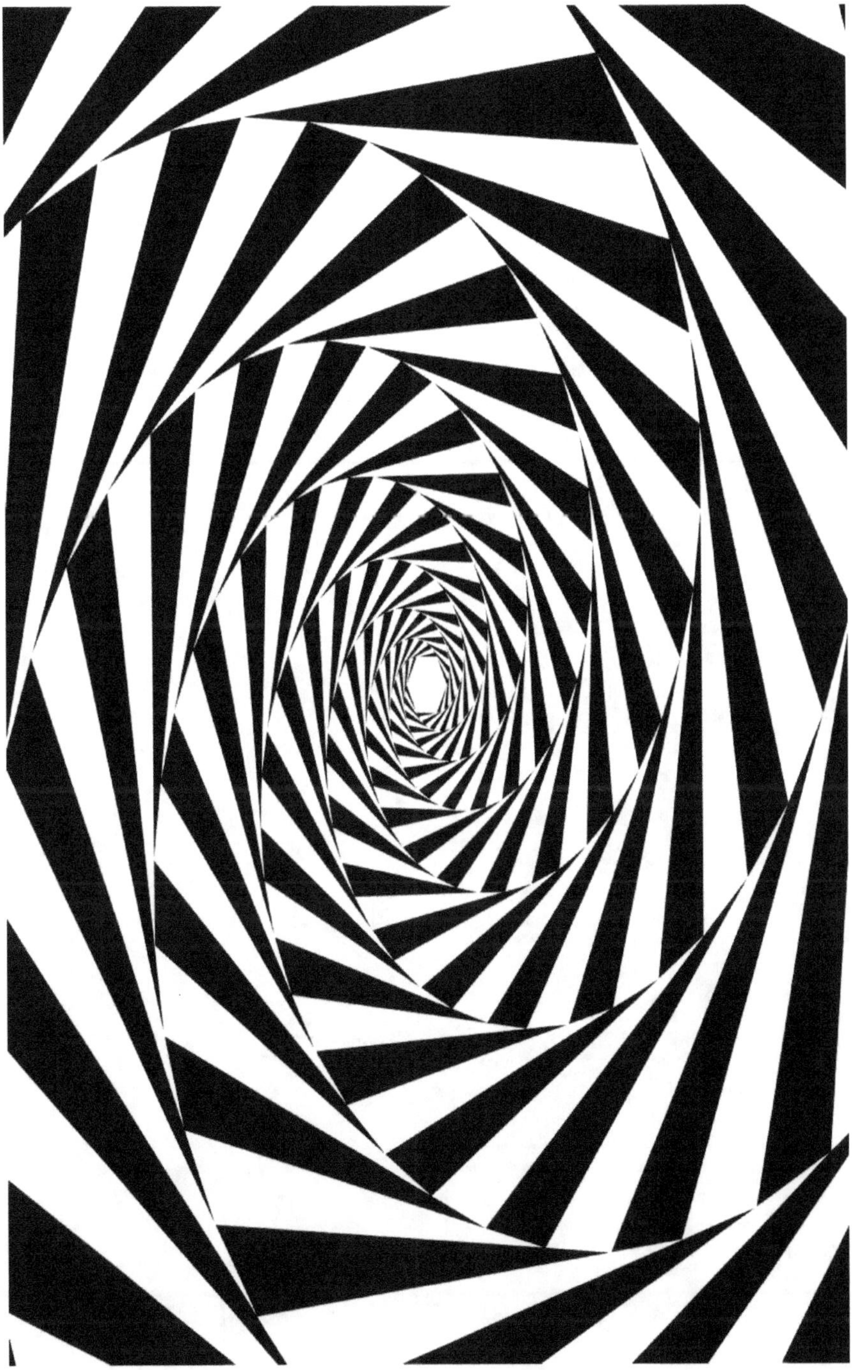

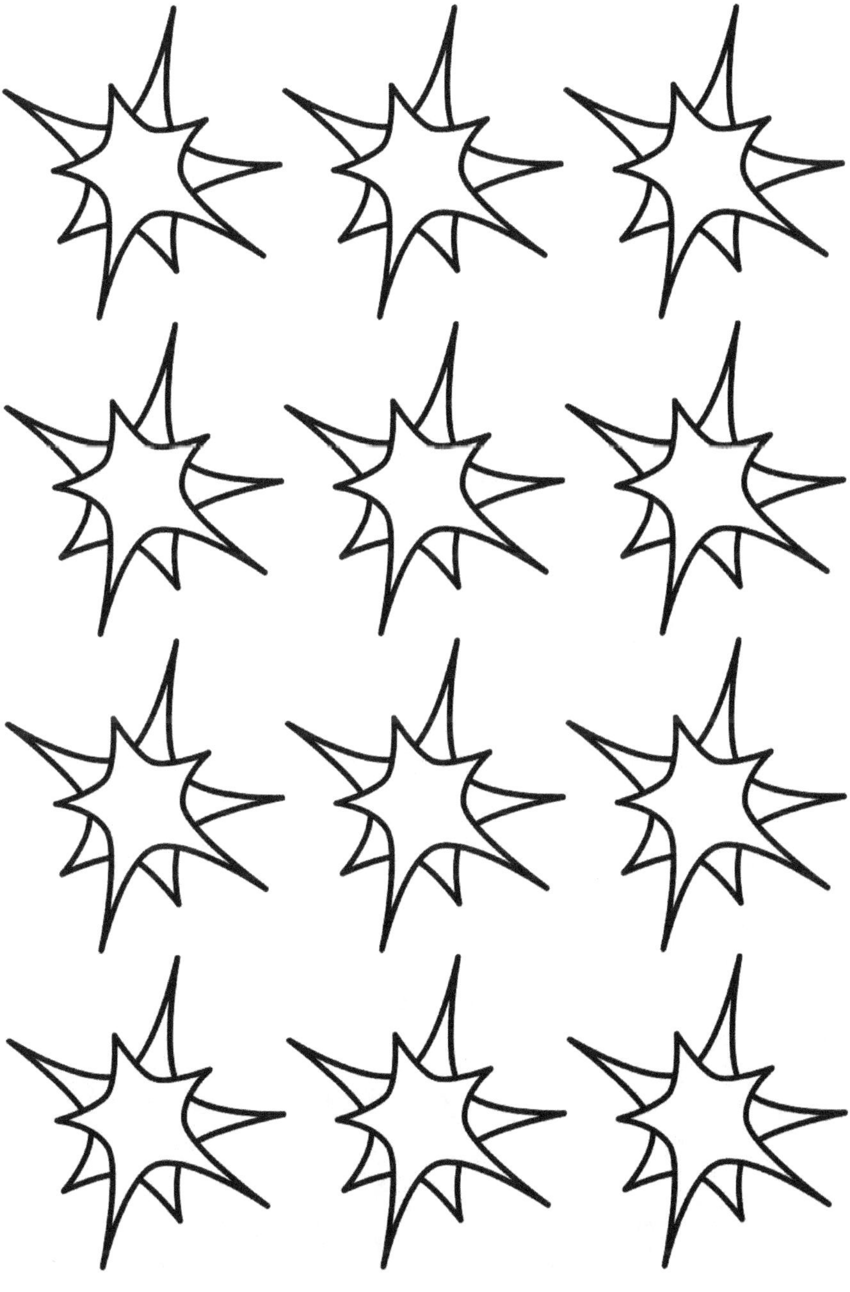

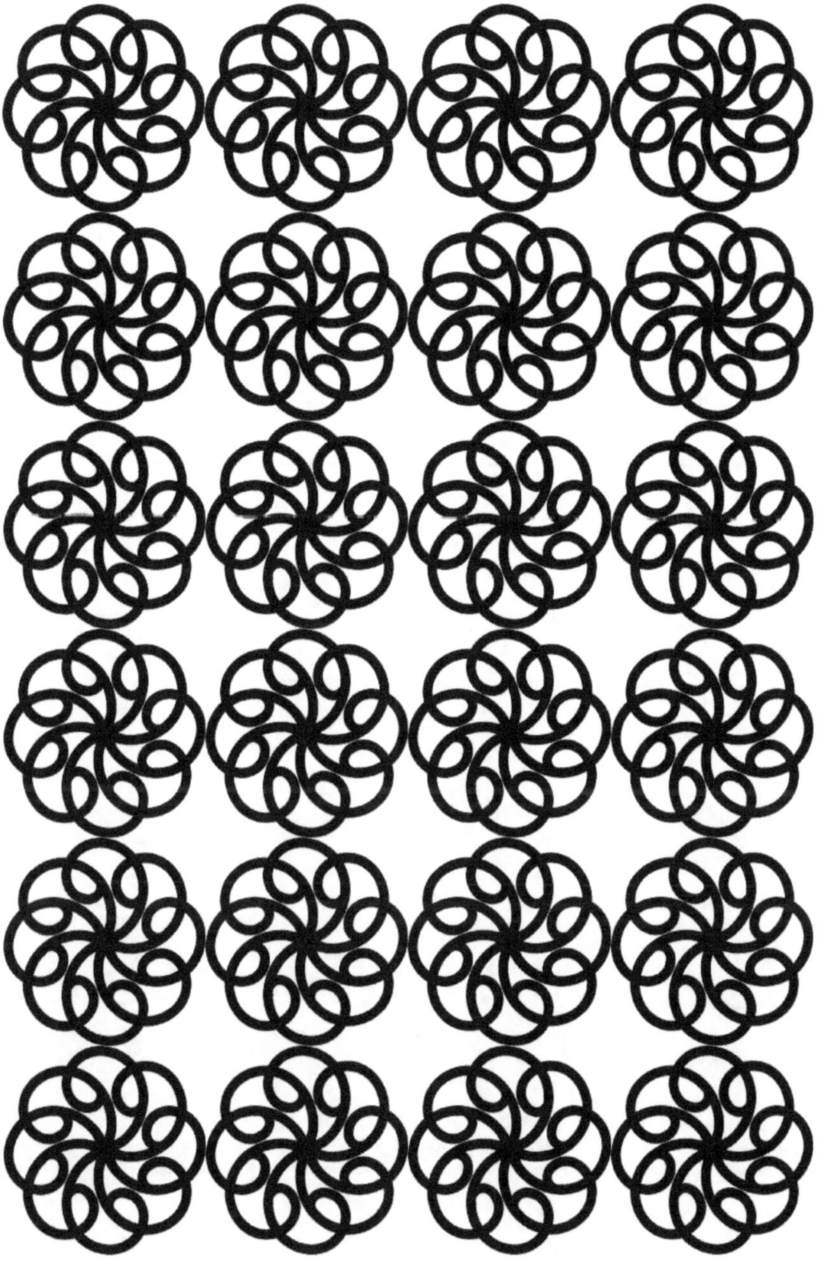

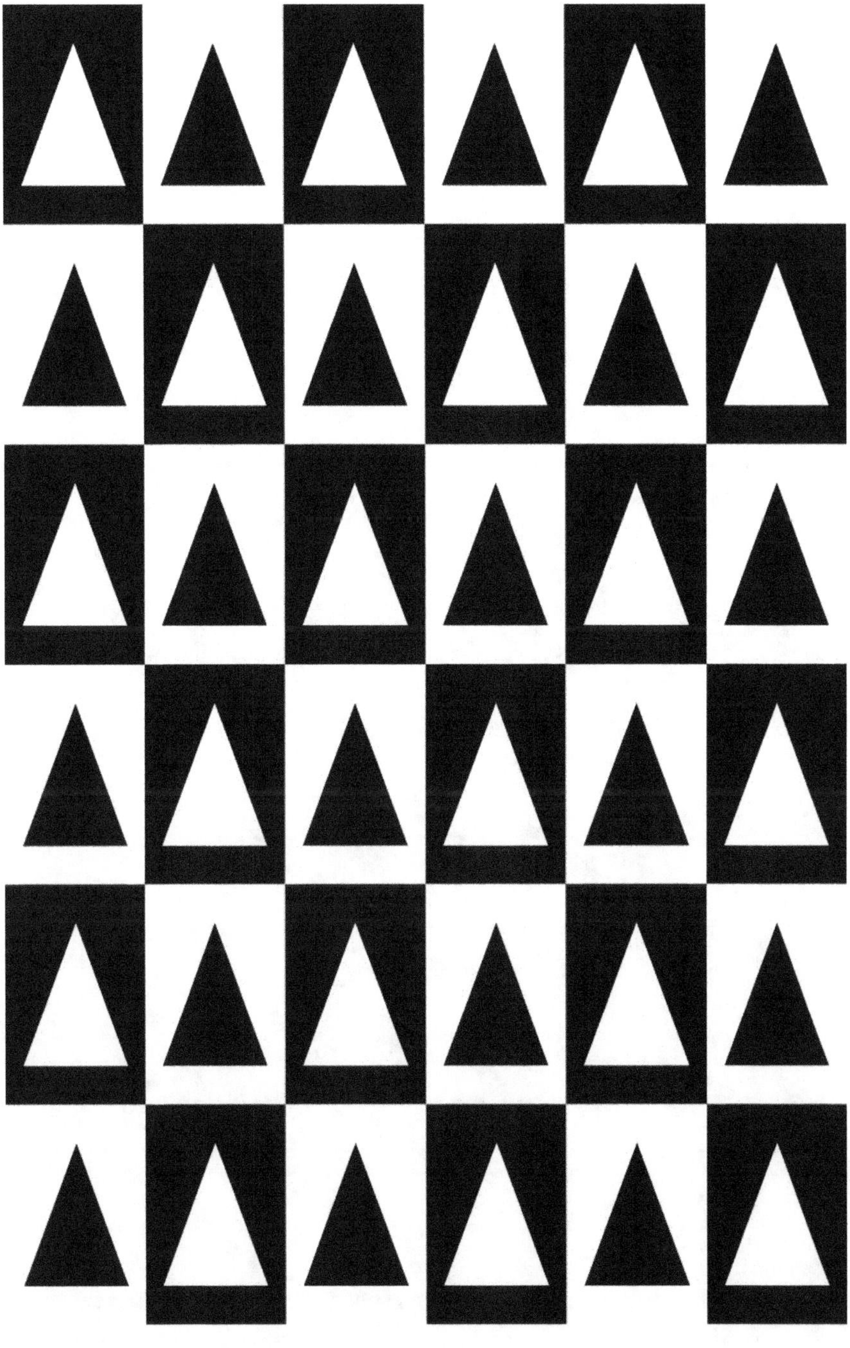

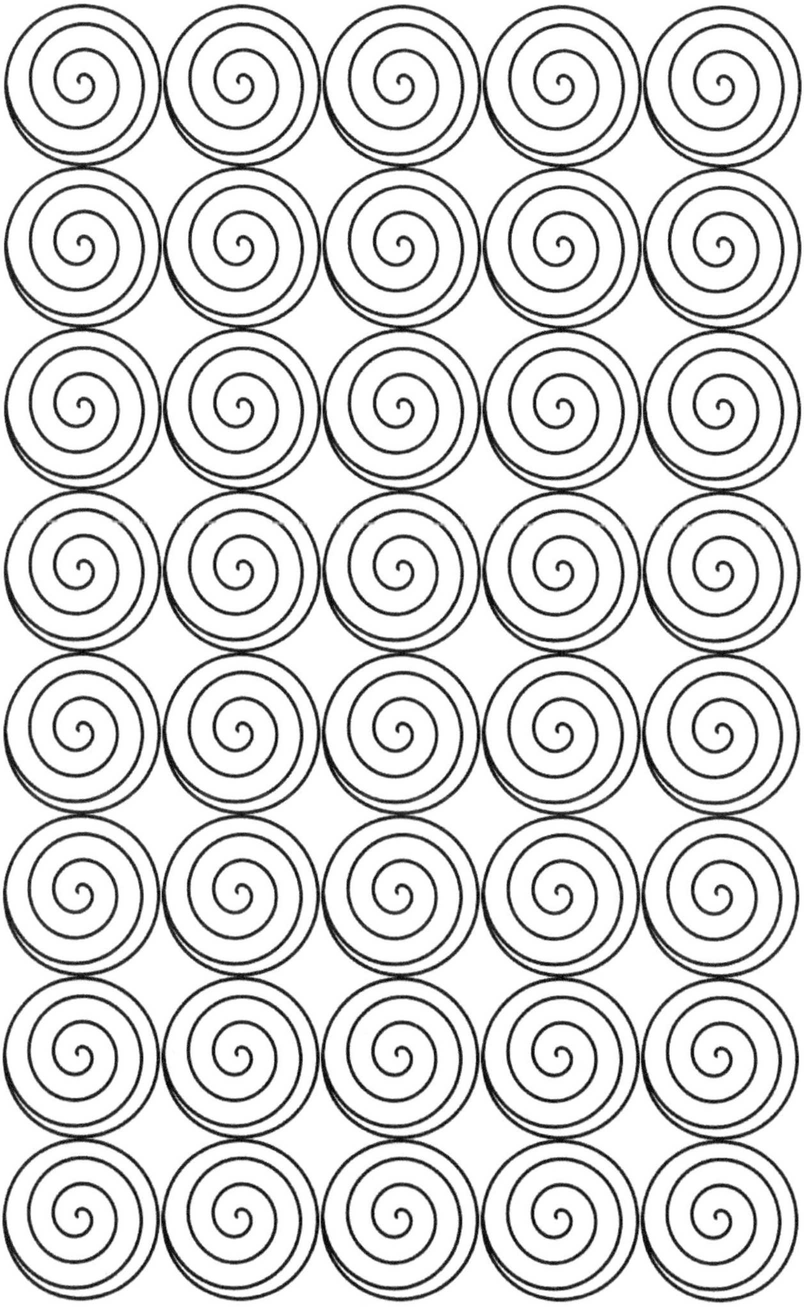

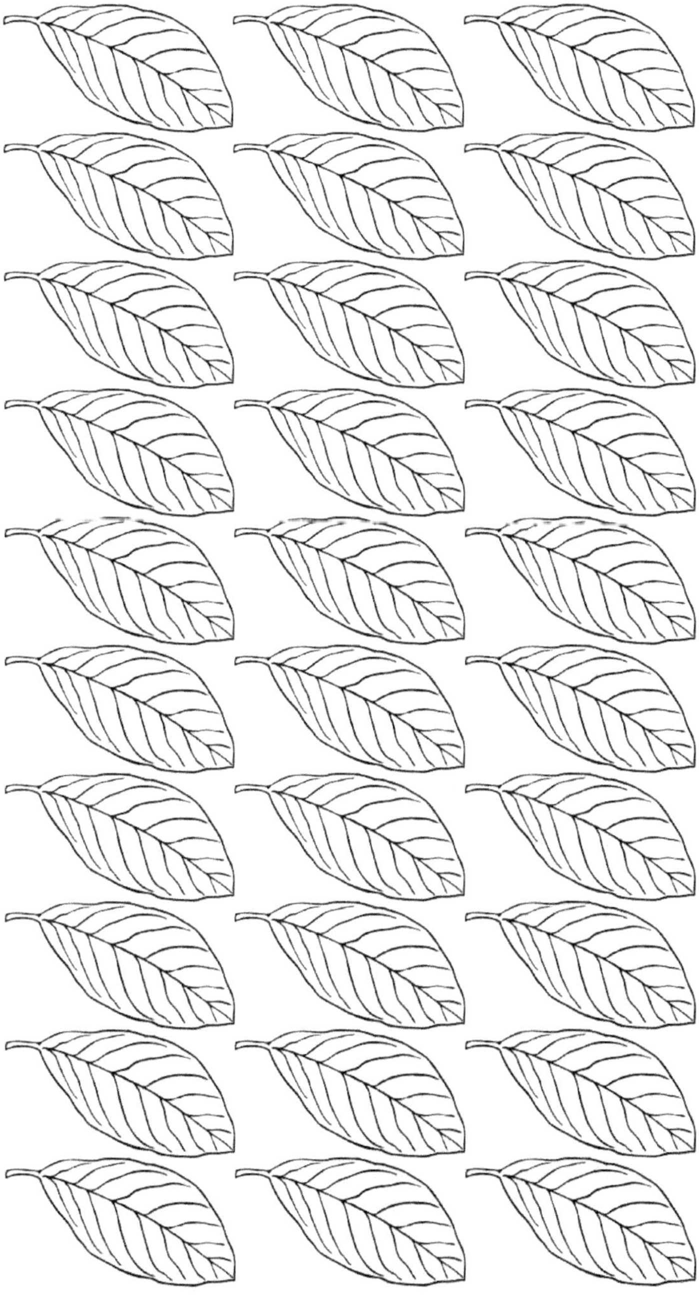

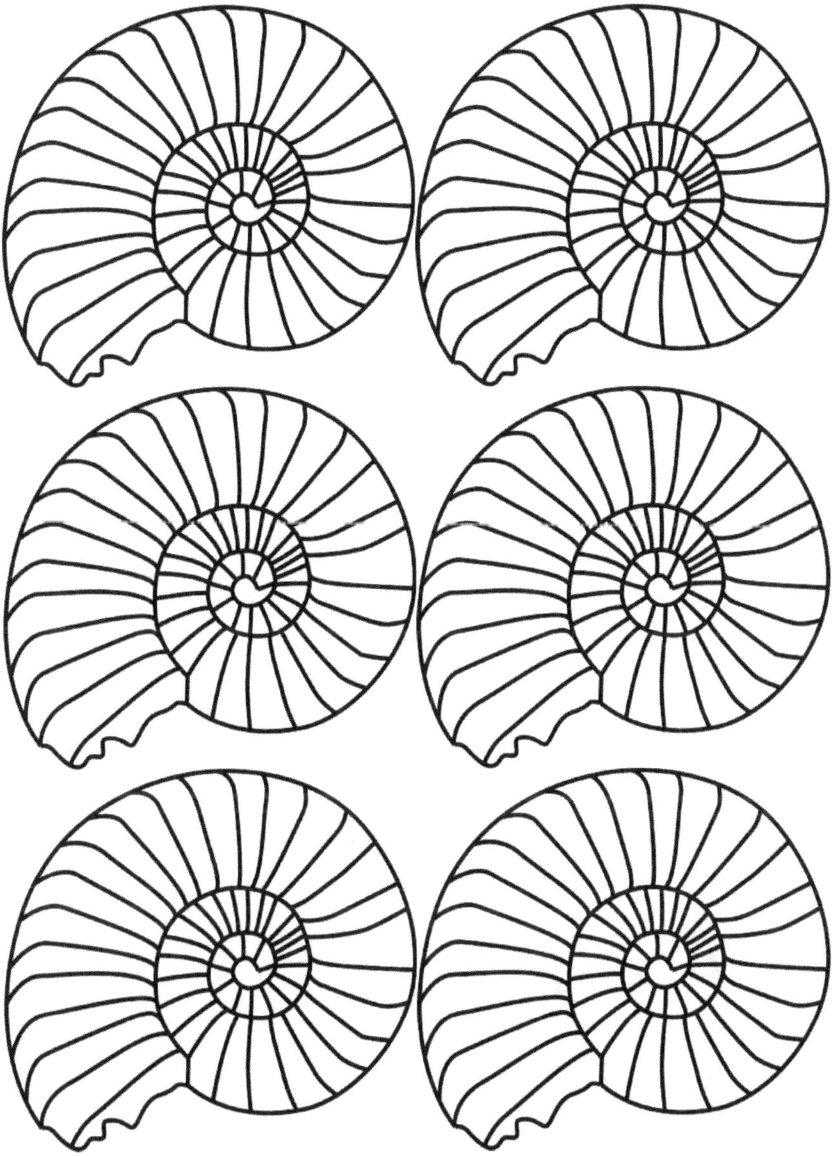

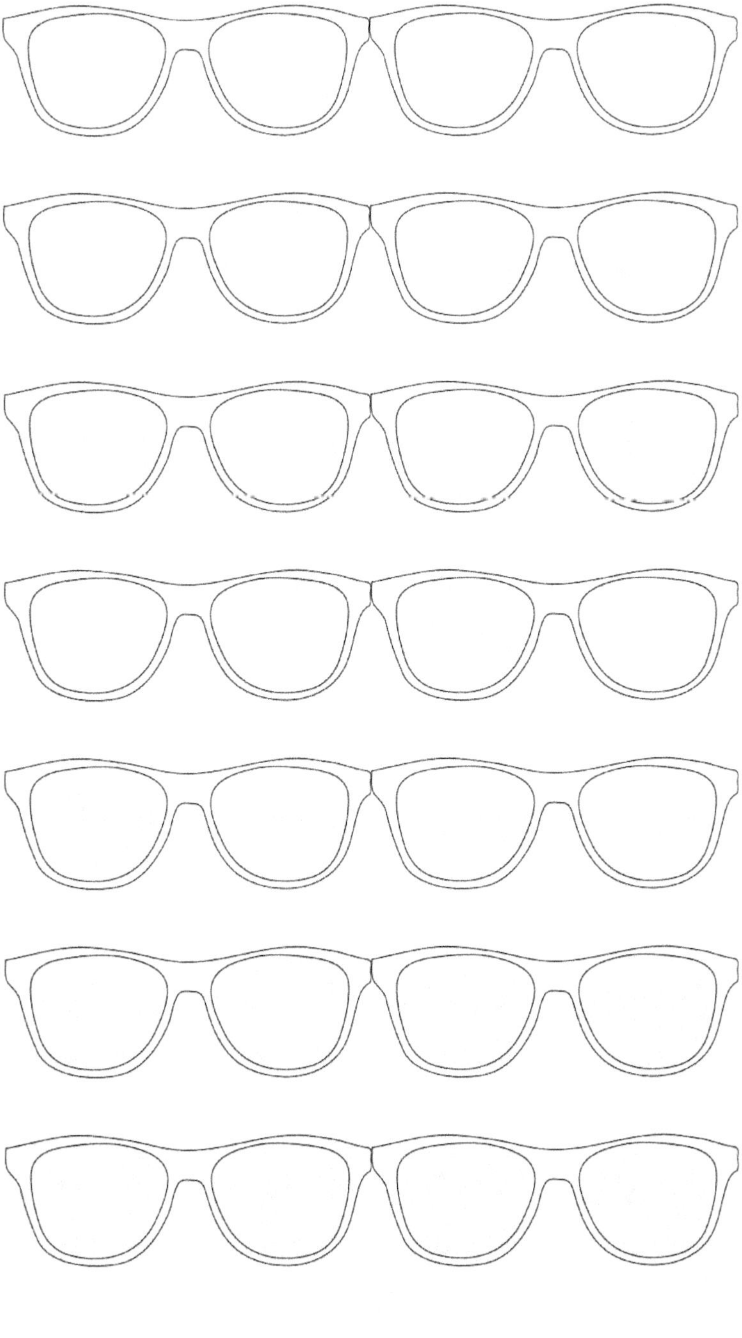

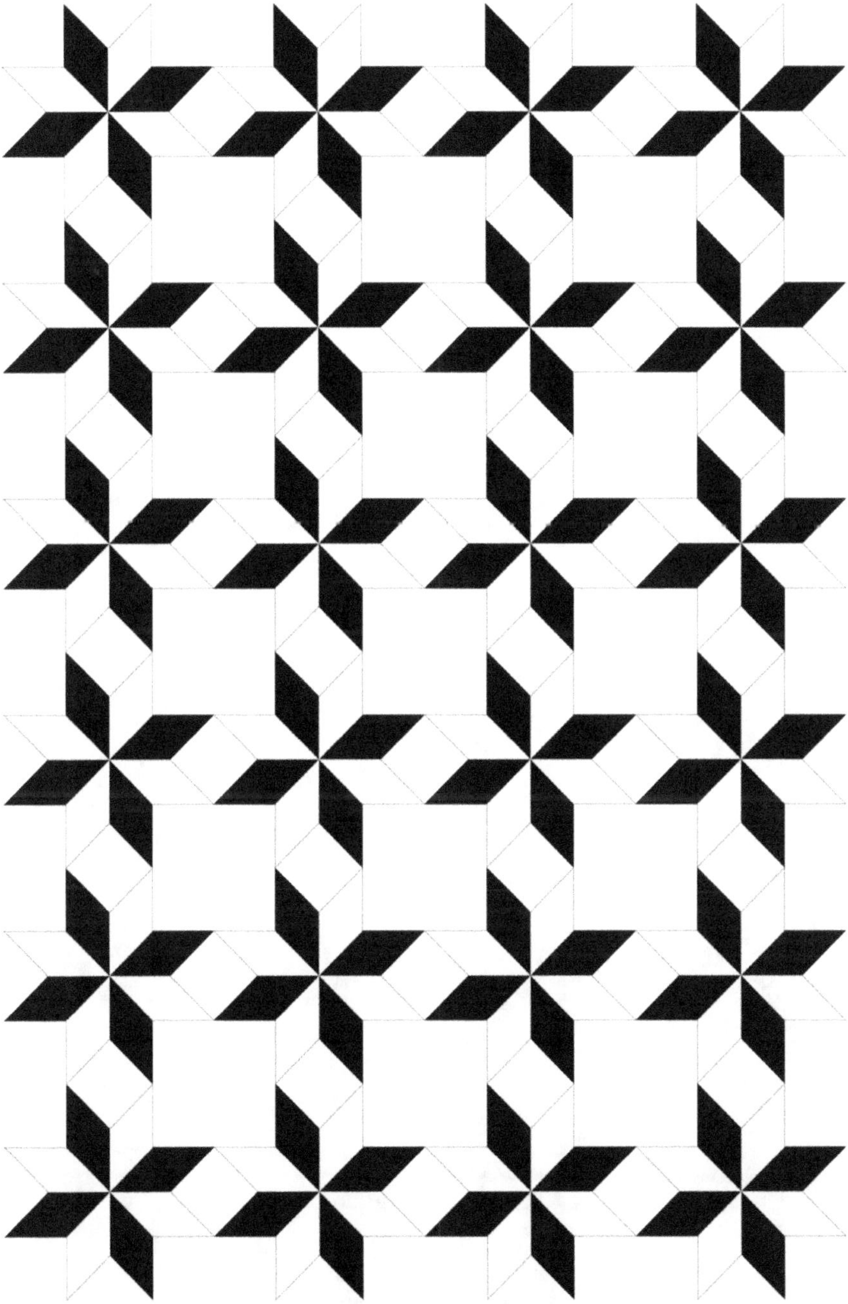

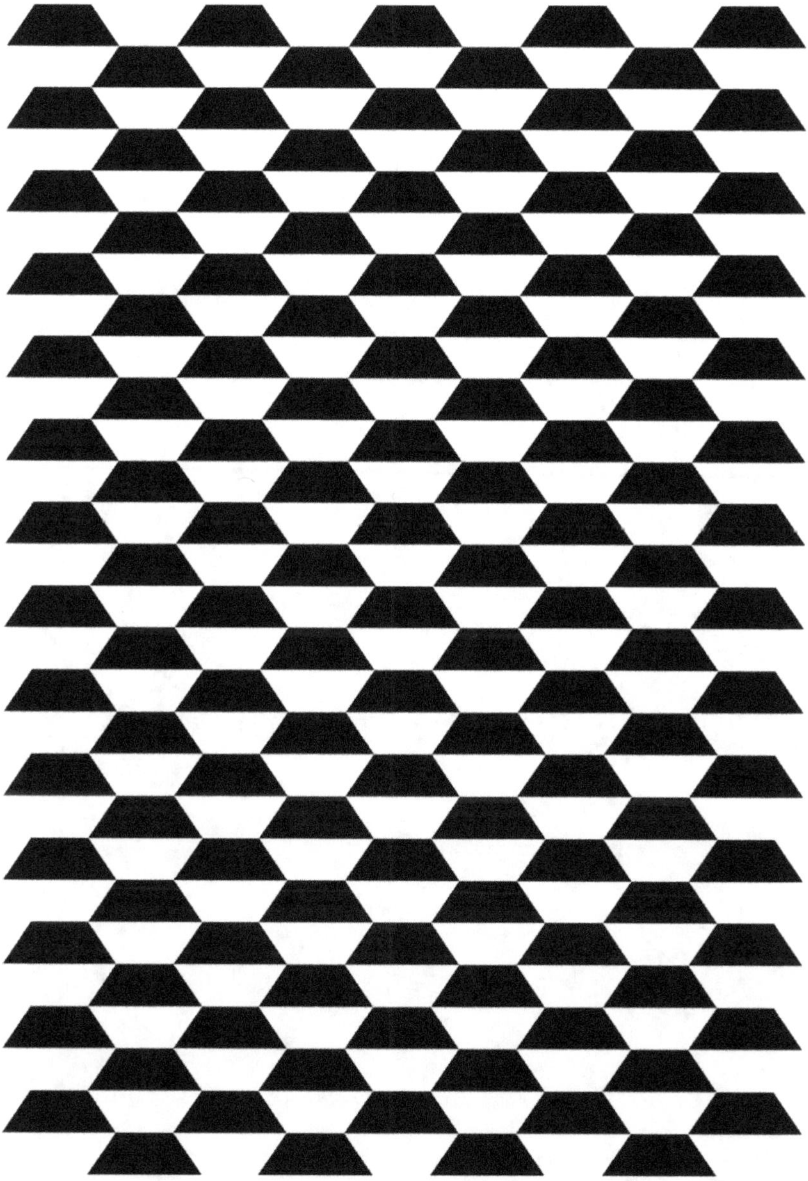

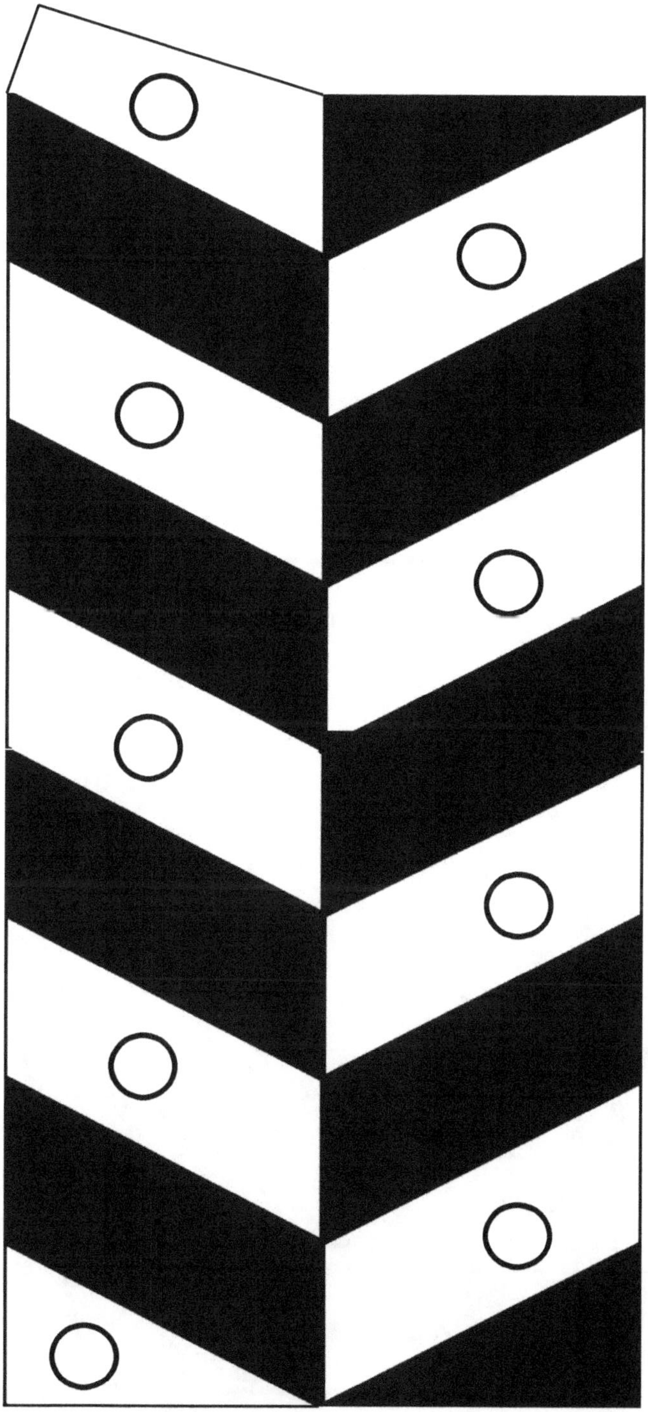

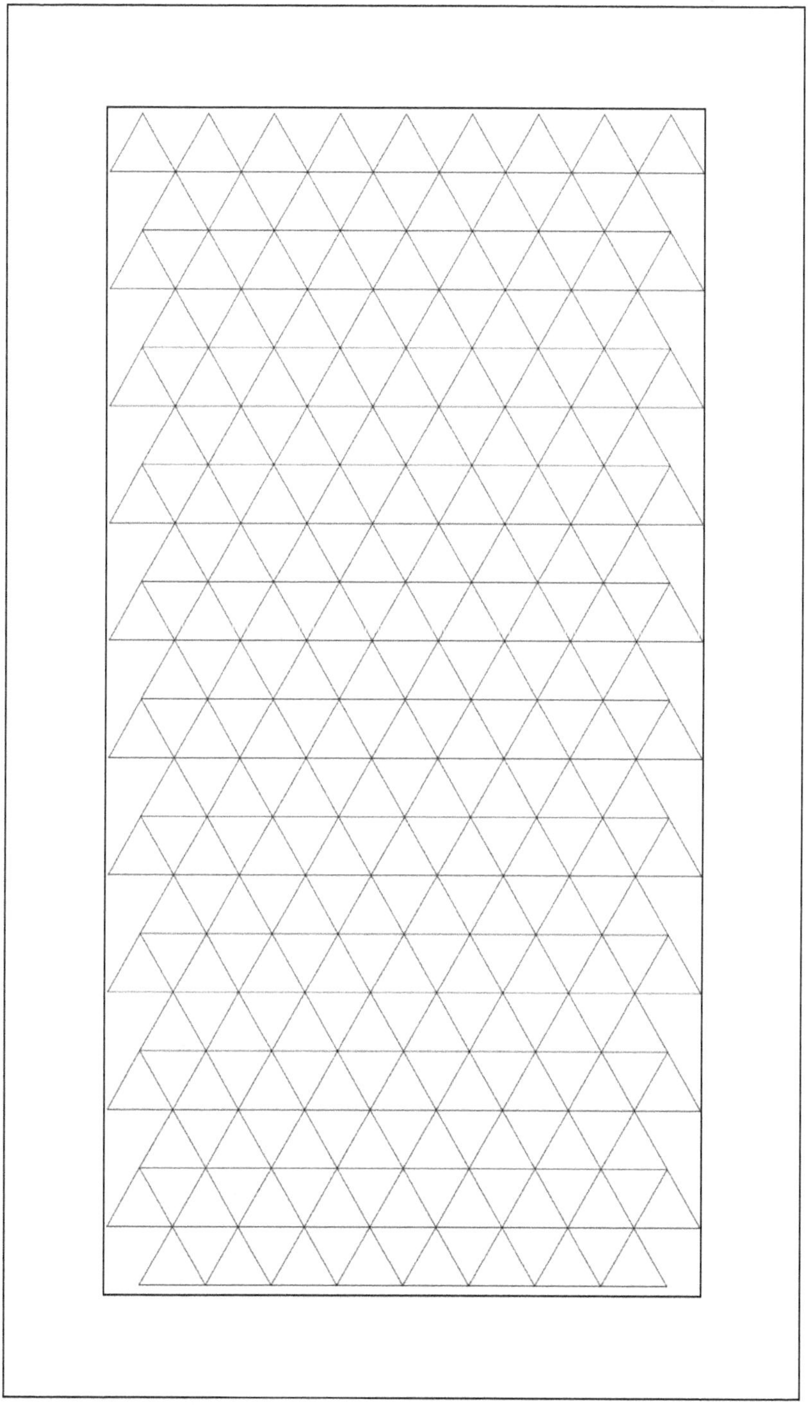

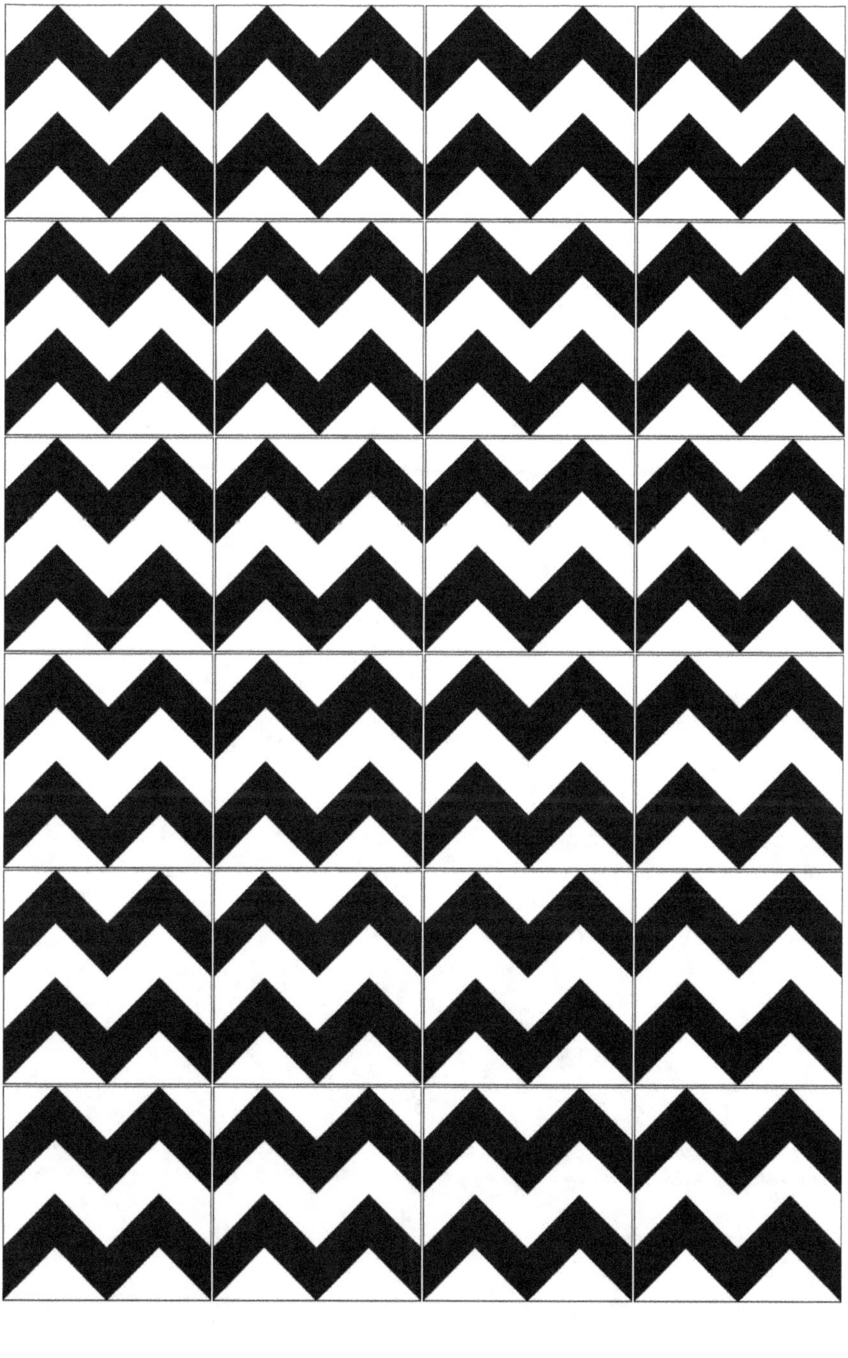

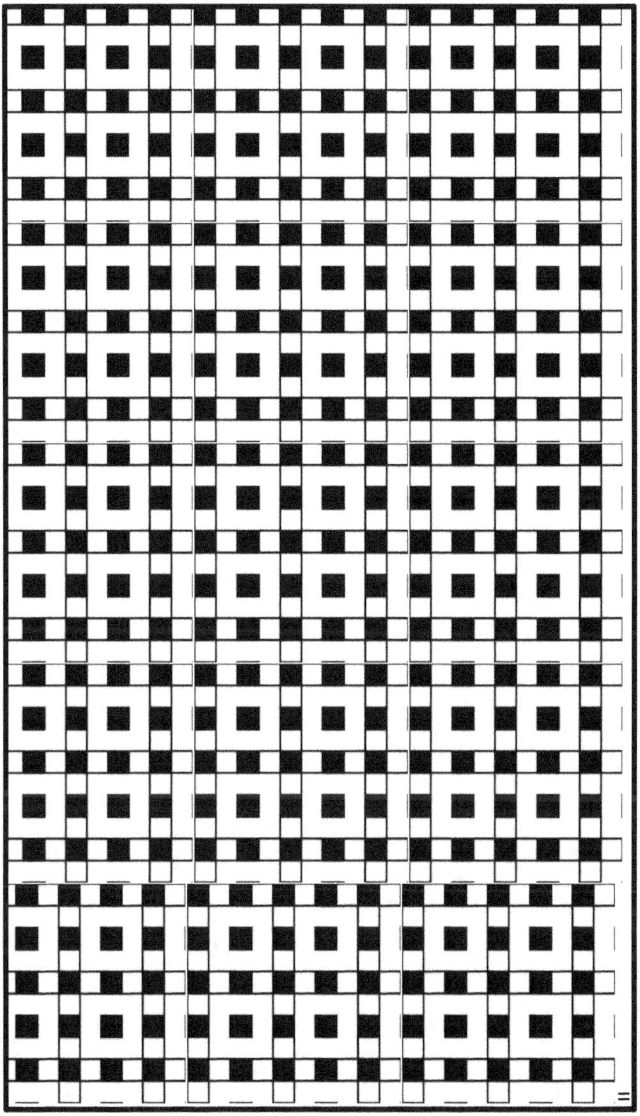

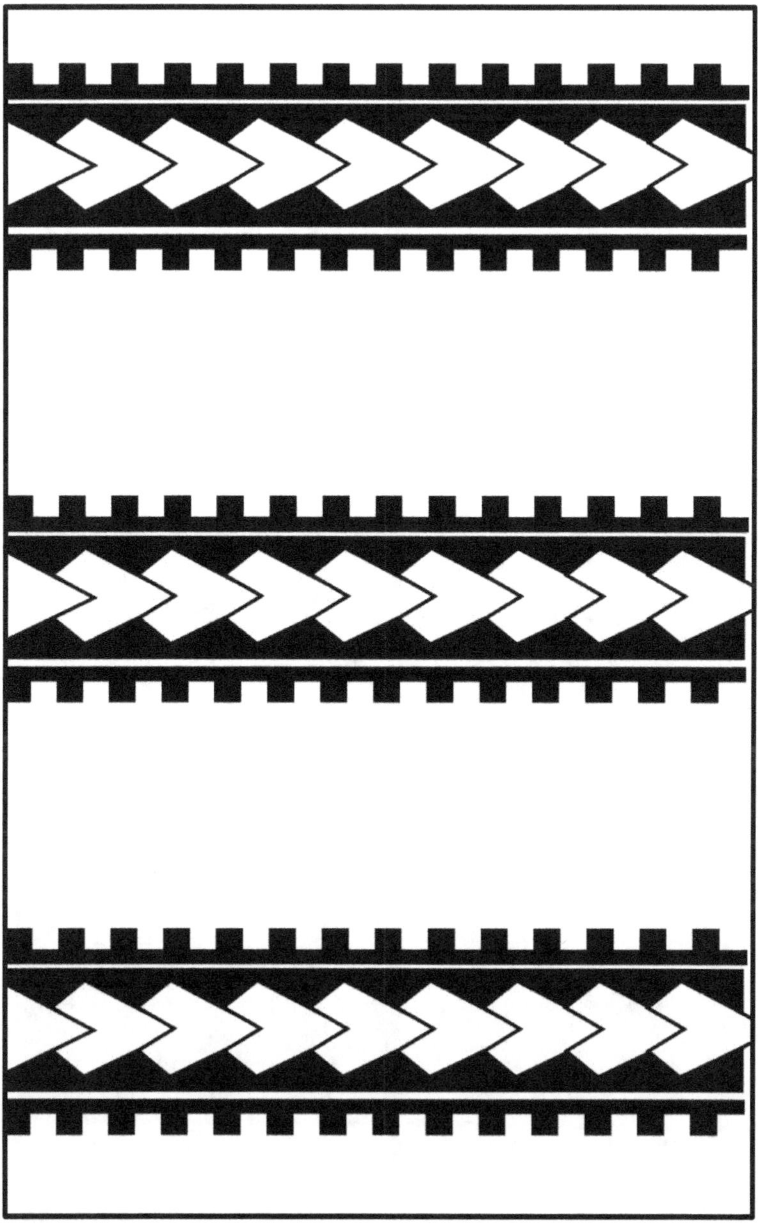

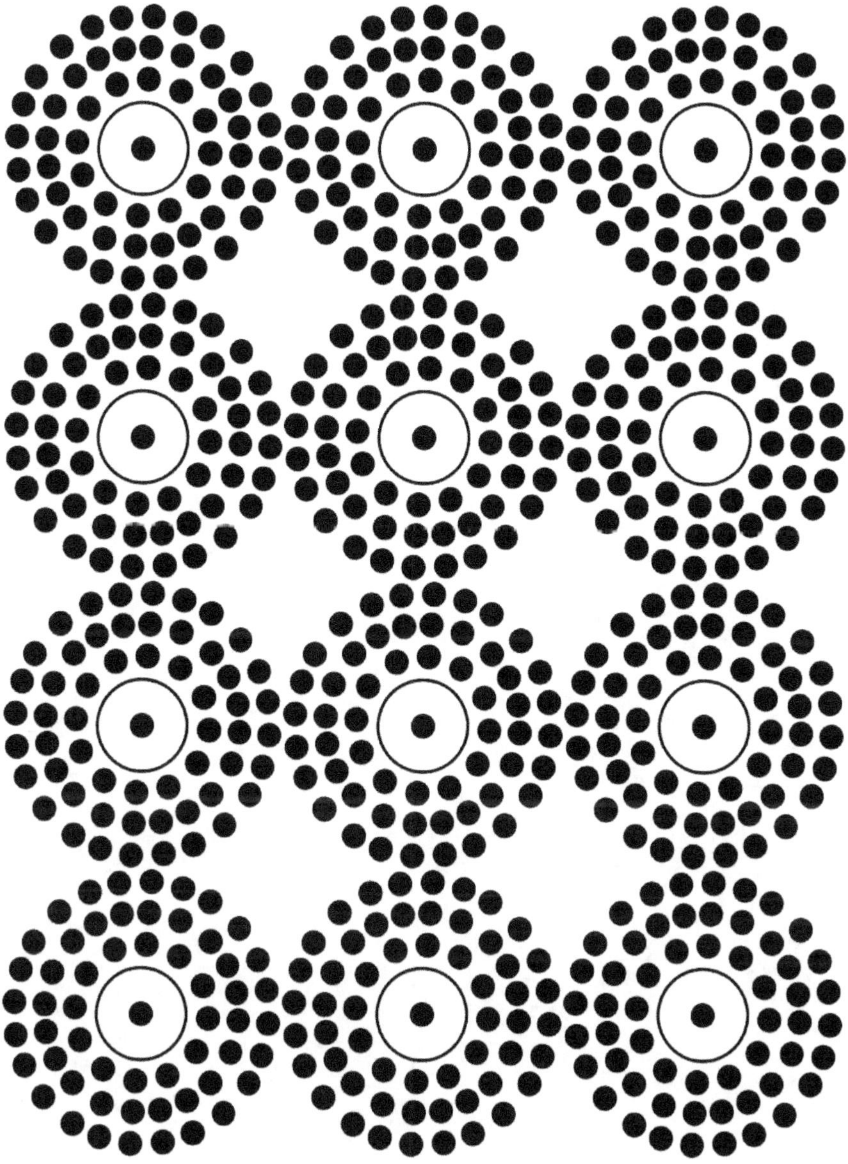

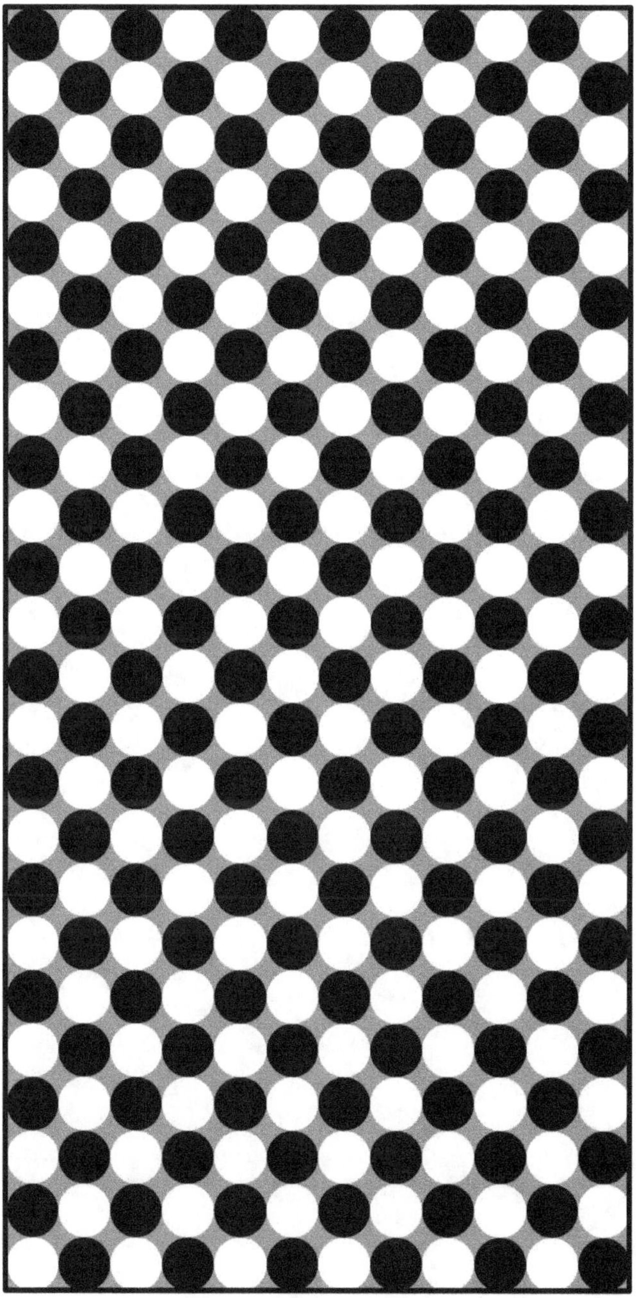

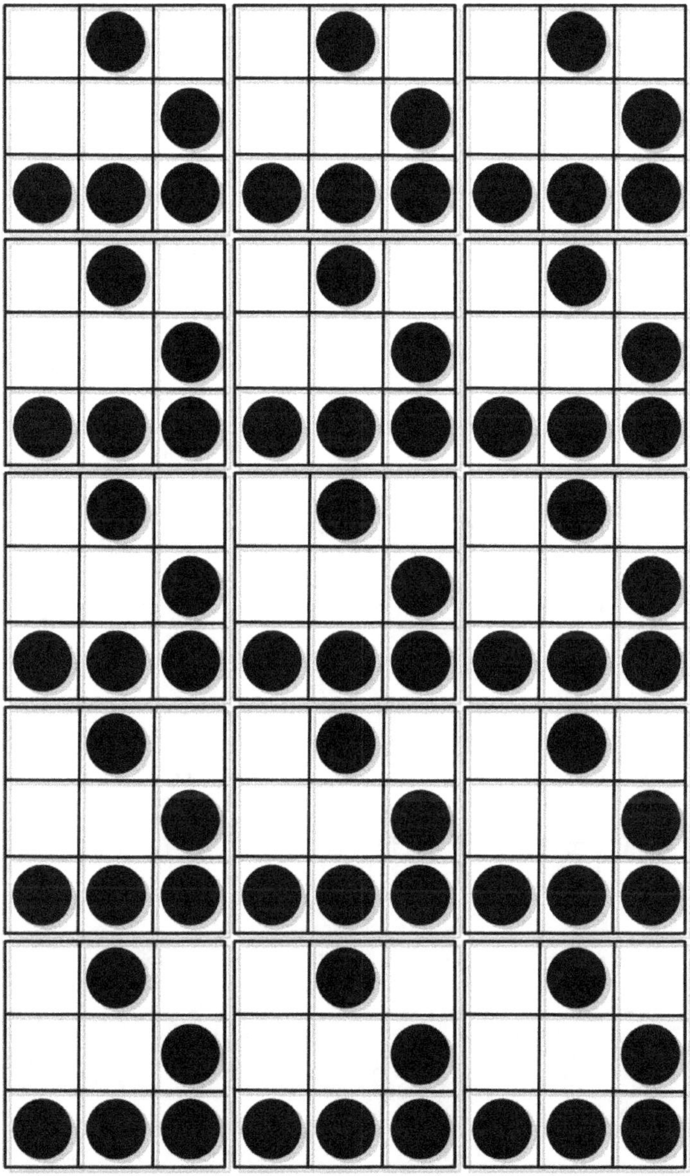

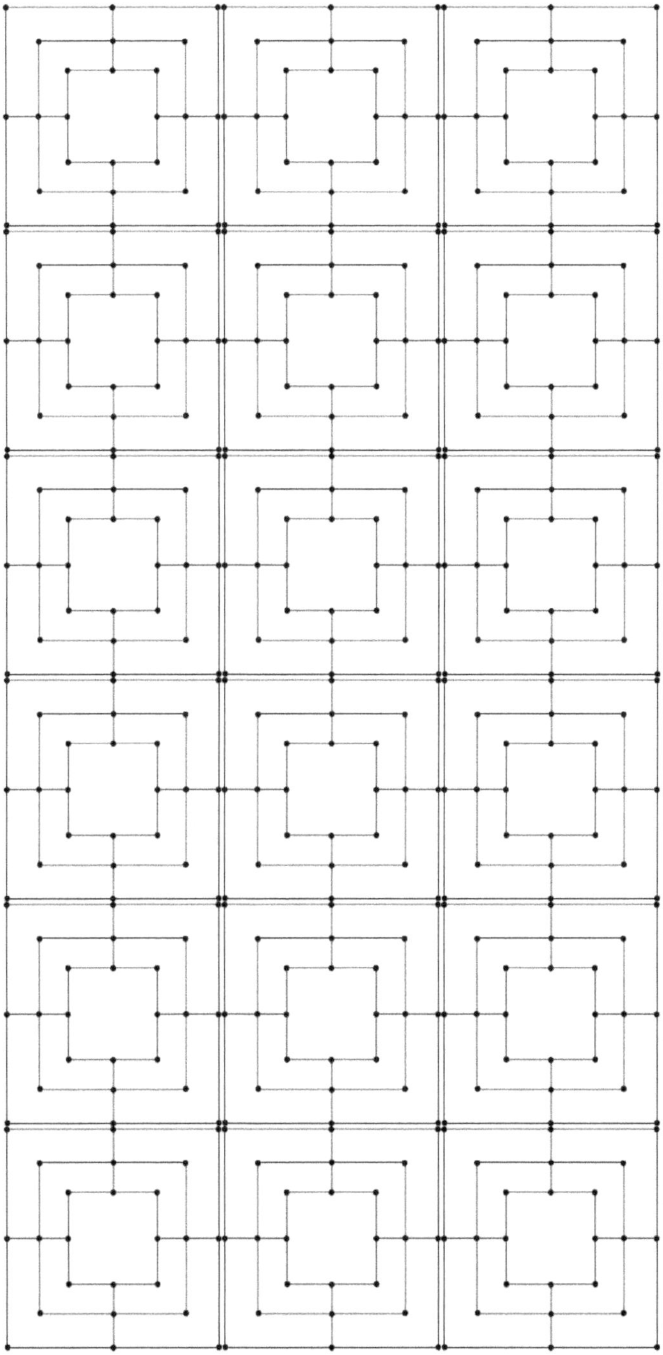

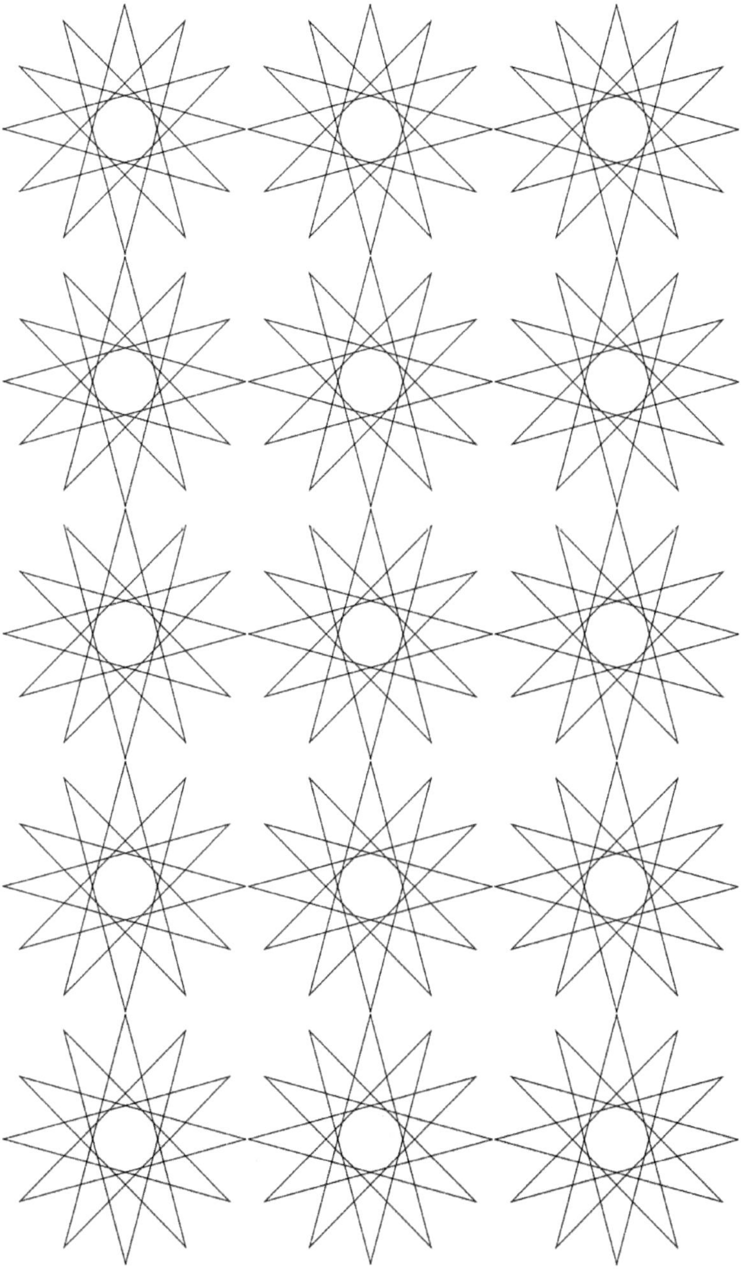

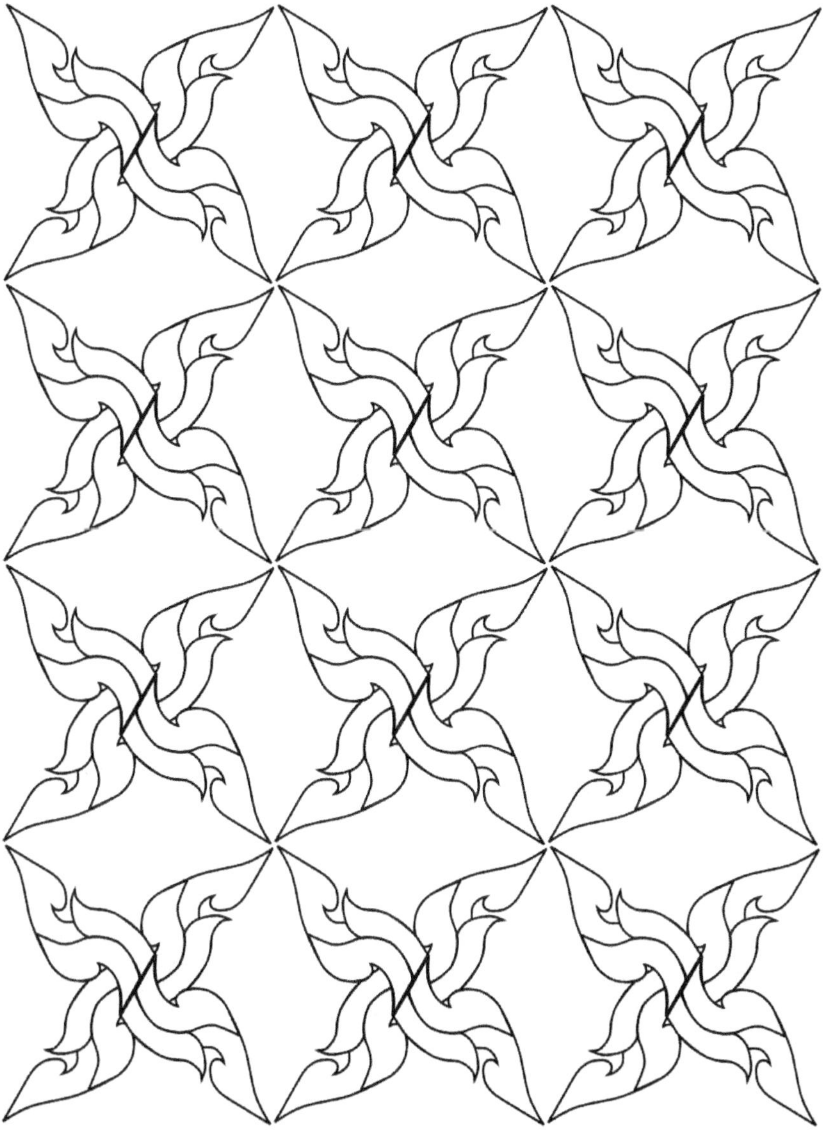

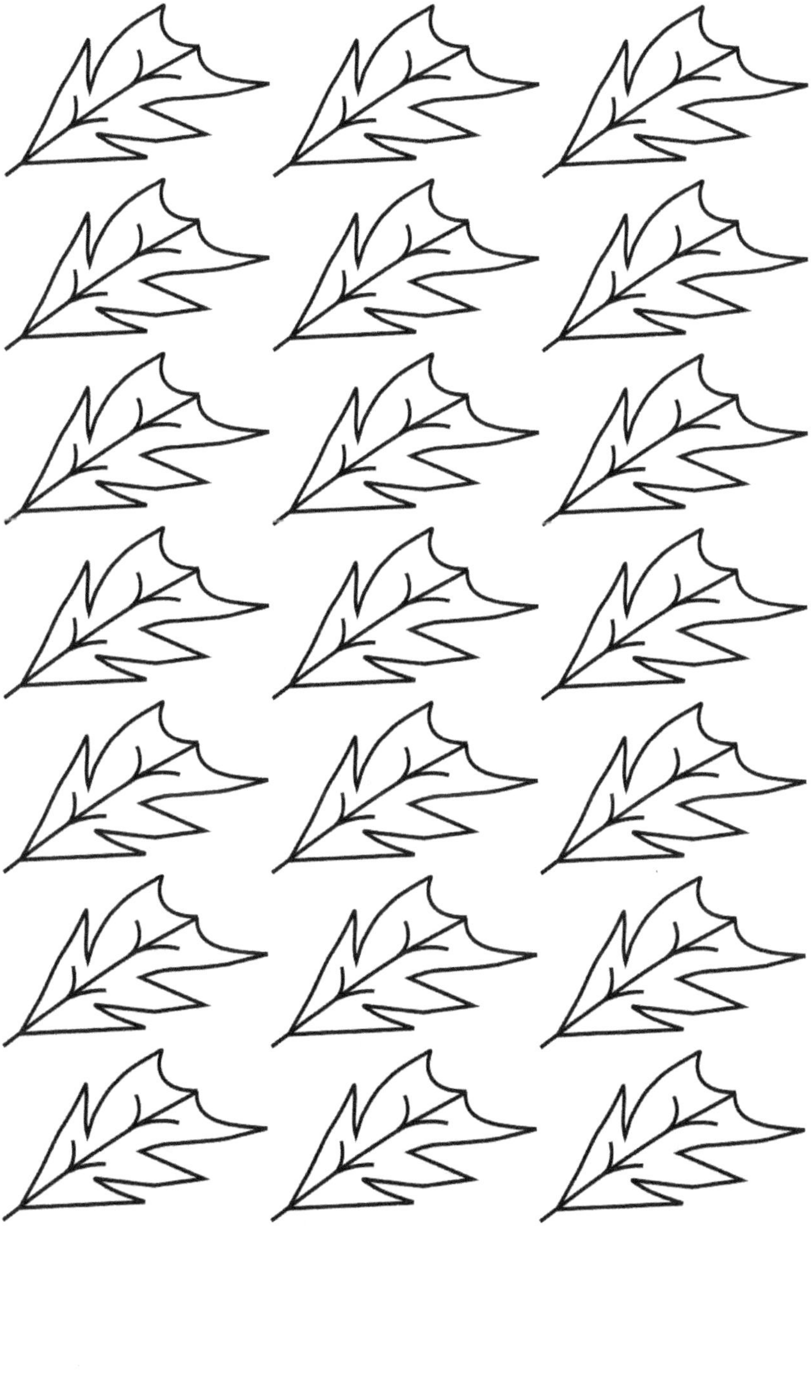

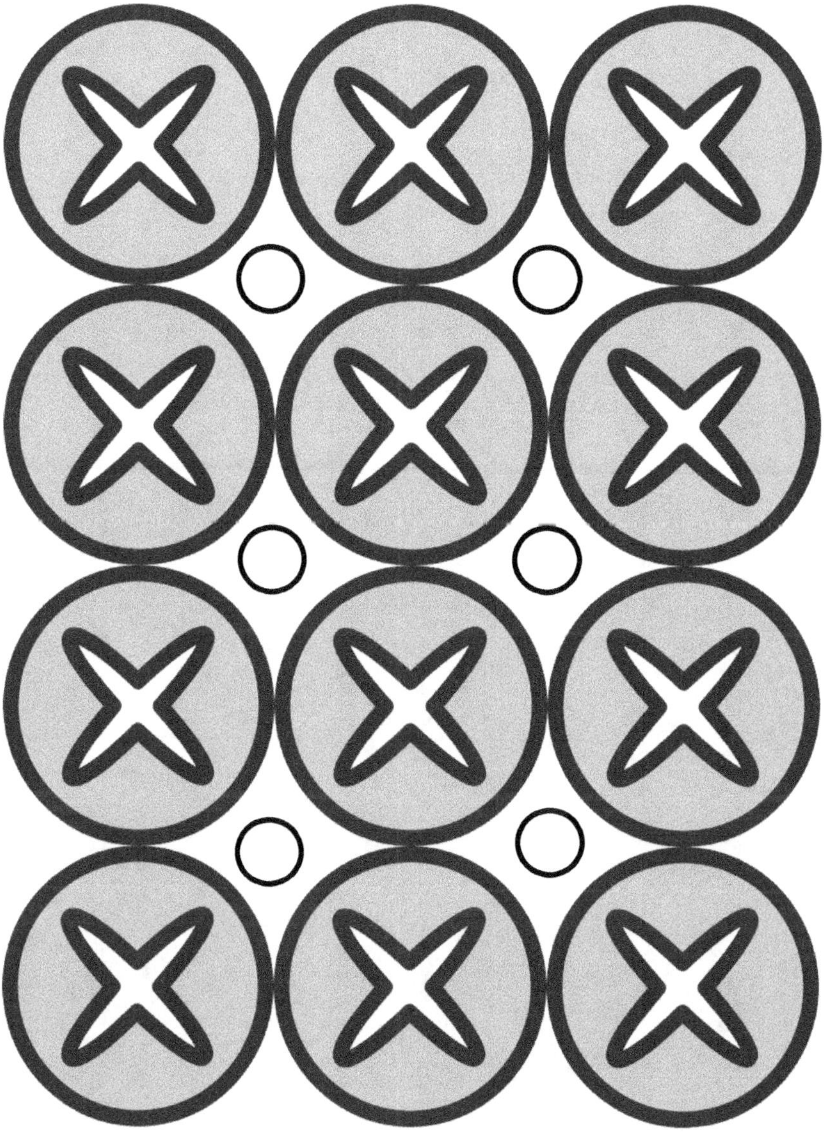

www.ingramcontent.com/pod-product-compliance
Lightning Source LLC
Chambersburg PA
CBHW070358190526
45169CB00003B/1038
* 9 7 8 1 5 3 2 8 2 1 6 4 6 *